I0436856

"Coffee Table Musings of the Da Vinci in Cowboy Boots"

Pithy Prose and Perspicacious Aphorisms

BY

PROF. HON. RANDOLPH M. HOWES, M.D., Ph.D.

Orthomolecular Surgical Scientist and Biochemist

Adjunct Assistant Professor of Plastic Surgery,

The Johns Hopkins Hospital, Baltimore, MD USA

Espaldon Professor of Plastic and Reconstructive Surgery,

University of Santo Tomas, Manila, Philippines

Adjunct Professor of Biological Sciences,

Southeastern Louisiana University

Professor of Surgery, Biophysics and Biochemistry,

Louisiana University of Medical Sciences

Vice Chancellor/Dean, Louisiana University of Medical Sciences

(Also holds an Honorary Doctorate of Humanities, SLU)

Copyright © 2009

Free Radical Publishing Co.

Kentwood, LA.

Howes, R. M. © 2009. Free Radical Publishing Co. Kentwood, LA

Order this book online at www.trafford.com
or email orders@trafford.com

Most Trafford titles are also available at major online book retailers.

© Copyright 2009 Prof. Hon. Randolph M. Howes M.D., Ph.D..
All rights reserved. No part of this publication may be reproduced, stored in a retrieval system, or
transmitted, in any form or by any means, electronic, mechanical, photocopying, recording, or
otherwise, without the written prior permission of the author.

Printed in Victoria, BC, Canada.

ISBN: 978-1-4269-2041-7

*Our mission is to efficiently provide the world's finest, most comprehensive book publishing
service, enabling every author to experience success. To find out how to publish your
book, your way, and have it available worldwide, visit us online at www.trafford.com*

Trafford rev. 12/28/09

 www.trafford.com

North America & international
toll-free: 1 888 232 4444 (USA & Canada)
phone: 250 383 6864 ♦ fax: 812 355 4082

Foreword

For over forty years, I've been absolutely amazed by the intellect, insight, humor and phenomenal energy of Randolph M. Howes. For me, our friendship has been inspiring and life changing. He is the Nietzsche of southeastern Louisiana. His genius operates on many levels. I've admired his talent, followed his path and witnessed his miracles. He even convinced me I might perform some of my own.

His credo in his own words:

> "I am the one who wishes to be studious,
> when others do not want to study,
> to be diligent, when others do not want to work
> and the one who remains curious for discovery,
> whilst others remain pacified.
> I am the doer.
> I can. I will. I must."

R. M. Howes, M.D., Ph.D.

5/25/04

Don't be put off by the pugnaciousness of this intellectual Cassius Clay, Randolph M. Howes speaks truth, the radical truth.

Robert C. Allen, M.D., Ph.D.
Professor, Creighton University School of Medicine, Department of
Pathology, Director, Creighton Medical Laboratories,
Omaha, NE USA

Short Biographical Sketch:

Prof. Hon. Randolph M. Howes M.D., Ph.D.

Dr. Howes was the first in the history of Tulane School of Medicine to be awarded a Doctorate of Medicine degree and a Ph.D. in Biochemistry at the same time. He was trained as a General surgeon and a Plastic surgeon at the prestigious Johns Hopkins Hospital, in Baltimore, Maryland. He was the first in the history of Johns Hopkins Hospital to obtain board eligibility in both general and plastic surgery in a six year period.

Dr. Howes invented the triple lumen venous catheter, which has been credited with helping save the lives of over 20 million critically ill patients worldwide. His catheter is the number one venous catheter in the world today and his name is well recognized in over 100 countries. He has been recognized as a humanitarian, visionary, entrepreneur, singer, songwriter, inventor and author. He received the Harper Award from the American College for Advancement in Medicine, served as their keynote speaker and his peers refer to him as "a walking encyclopedia on oxygen metabolism."

He is currently doing extensive research on cures for cancer and heart disease and developing revolutionary treatment modalities. He has written 13 books (over 5,000 pages) over the past 6 years on the subject of oxygen metabolism, as it relates to protection from cancer, heart disease, diabetes, malaria, HIV/AIDS, Alzheimer's disease, aging and arthritis. He has written many scientific and medical papers and has lectured nationally and internationally.

His research has shown that currently popular antioxidant vitamins, such as vitamins A & E, can be harmful and that oxygen free radicals protect us from bacterial, fungal and viral infections and act in the control of cancerous growths. He has developed an effective breakthrough and an inexpensive singlet oxygen generating system, from orthomolecular agents, for the treatment of cancer. He is passionate about his research and strives to have his discoveries at the patient's bedside in his lifetime.

During the compilation of Dr. Howes' research books on oxygen metabolism, he recorded his aside musings for both informative and entertainment purposes. This book represents a five year collection of these pithy and perspicacious sayings. It is his sincere hope that they are enjoyed by all readers. His sardonic humor is akin to Ambrose Bierce but his intellectual capacity ranks with the best that science and medicine have today. In a 1978 article about Dr. Howes, a reporter called him "a da Vinci in Cowboy Boots" and the sobriquet stuck. So, sit back, relax, laugh a little and enjoy. This could be the best book in the history of ever! These "sardonic nuggets" are like potato chips…you can't have just one.

For more author information visit: www.iwillfindthecure.org or www.thepundit.com.

Howes, R. M. U.T.O.P.I.A. - Unified Theory of Oxygen Participation in Aerobiosis.

© 2004. Free Radical Publishing Co. Kentwood, LA

"A mind constrained by misleading doggerel
is difficult to open
and impedes rational consideration
concerning emotional topics.
Ergo, it is necessary to distinguish fact
from manipulated myth,
to dispel generally accepted inaccuracies
and to challenge the power of the uninformed."

R. M. Howes, M.D., Ph.D.

3/4/04

"The cell's intracellular cytoplasmic sea is
an ocean of symphonic motion awash with
incomprehensible complexity."

R. M. Howes, M.D., Ph.D.

1/24/04

"Oxygen: aerobic life's lone elixir."

R.M. Howes, M.D., Ph.D.

8/04/04

"With freshmanic amazement and sophomoric curiosity,
I study the hidden wonders and arcane secrets
of the aerobic cell.
What my peers see as a metabolic melee and
free radical fracas,
I view as a molecular marvel of unparalleled design.
Yet, it is emblazoned with an unmistakable and
splendid imprint,
that is common throughout
our cosmos:
the signature of the electromagnetic field. "

R. M. Howes, M.D., Ph.D.

7/11/04

"The electron never rests.
Nonetheless, oxygen occasionally naps,
until enlivened by an
electron-volt jolt."

R. M. Howes, M.D., Ph.D.

7/11/04

"The raw materials needed to construct a man are
worth less than
five dollars of basic chemical components.
Yet, when properly oxygenated, hydrated, nourished and
assembled,
they form entities of value beyond estimation,
which we love and call
'self
and
our fellow man'."

R. M. Howes, M.D., Ph.D.

7/11/04

"A long, long time ago, on a tiny, insignificant
planet called Earth,
its primordial broth, bathed a biochemical gumbo,
irradiated it with sunlight and lightening bolts,
brought it to a boil,
let it cool and TAH-DAH!
A replicative molecule was spawned. Being educable,
over millennia it overcame narcosis and became aware
that it was aware….aware of itself.
Narcissism rapidly ensued and it became obsessed
with self-replication.
The hardy helix hastily scaled the phylogenetic tree,
crawling through you and slithering over me.
Willing to make all sacrifices, it now offers up its human host,
to the god of immortality to feed its mania and
to secure the dubious title of
"cancer."

R. M. Howes, M.D., Ph.D.

6/18/04

"God said, 'Let there be light .'
and singlet oxygen emitted its photon
into the chemical nightscape,
illuminating the cell's dark reactions.
And the light was good.
Now excited carbonyls and oxygen impart their
photon energy
bringing about the perpetual resurrection of the electron;
thus, empowering the momentous cycle of light
and the great circle of life."

R. M. Howes, M.D., Ph.D.

6/11/04

"The living/breathing cell is a cornucopia of
exciting electron affinities,
a thermodynamic treasure trove of biochemical
perplexities and
a temple of uncertainty for medical and scientific curiosity.
The cellular conundrum is a deliciously clever concoction
cooked up by an all-knowing Riddler."

R. M. Howes, M.D., Ph.D.

6/18/04

"Medicine's history and its practice teaches us that physicians and scientists alike, can be blinded by obviousness and entrapped by ignorance."

R. M. Howes, M.D., Ph.D.

5/2/04

"Future's shape is sculpted by the persistent kneading hands of the impossible dreamer."

R. M. Howes, M.D., Ph.D.

5/2/04

"To be possessed with the gift to see the unseen or
to know the unknown, even for a fleeting second,
can be an unparalleled blessing,
rife with reward or
a daunting flash of peril,
the immediate result of which will be determined, not by
ultimate truth, but by the amplitude of reactionaries."

R. M. Howes, M.D., Ph.D.

5/25/04

"Remember, I am the one who wishes to be studious,
when others do not want to study,
to be diligent, when others do not want to work
and the one who remains curious for discovery,
whilst others remain pacified.
I am the doer.
I can. I will. I must."

R. M. Howes, M.D., Ph.D.

5/25/04

"The achievers drink
from the endless stream of opportunity
and bathe in the waters of wisdom
to heal
their wounds of criticism."

R. M. Howes, M.D., Ph.D.

5/3/04

"Even though our oral cavity and gastrointestinal tract are
teeming
with microbial life, we maintain healthy homeostasis.
Self-cure overcomes nature's insults, along with man's
nostrums
and levels the playing field for crystal therapy, urine drinking,
cupping, magnets, acupuncture, hexing, Western medicine
and the like. Medicine's recorded history teaches that,
in spite of man's meddlesome tendencies,
we are bolstered and sustained by self-cure
and its best buddy,
placebo."

R. M. Howes, M.D., Ph.D.

8/12/04

In our living state,
we are bounded by space and time.
Death extricates us from the confines of our skins,
thus, coalescing our essence with the spirit of endless space.
Our quietus frees us from the stressful restraints of time,
allowing us to frolic in infinity.

R.M. Howes, M.D., Ph.D.

8/21/04

"Excytology, the study of excited states, will thread the
scientific needle of truth,
which we will use to pierce the toughened hide
of the bloated, corpulent body
of medical ignorance,
in our quest for cures."

R. M. Howes, M.D., Ph.D.

5/27/04

"It would require Occam's bush-hog to cut away the fluff and gratuitous academic verbosity in today's scientific publications."

R. M. Howes, M.D., Ph.D.

5/25/04

"I must resuscitate oxygen's embattled image and effectuate the renaissance of its aristocratic attributes."

R. M. Howes, M.D., Ph.D.

5/4/04

"Aerobic life is choreographed by its oxygen instructor to perform the dance of the electron."

R. M. Howes, M.D., Ph.D.

2/25/04

"Singlet oxygen is spawned from the erotic mating ritual between stately hydrogen peroxide and perky hypochlorite. From this molecular true romance, is born the excited singlet love-child, which, within micro-seconds, rises to be a great leader
of electrons."

R. M. Howes, M.D., Ph.D.

5/26/04

"Obfuscation of scientific truth
by the deceptive smoke of meaningless associations
and the arcane mirrors of manipulated data
must be eschewed.
We must demand scientific exactitude."

R. M. Howes, M.D., Ph.D.

8/17/04

"Relative to oxygen metabolism,
the most damaging chain reaction that occurs,
is the uncontrolled dispersal of misinformation and
the perpetuation of erroneous conclusions."

R. M. Howes, M.D., Ph.D.

8/21/04

"Within the matrix of the virtual nano-world of cellular
signaling, oxygen's multiple personalities go about
their intricate peripatetic tasks, with an arrogant assurance
earned over eons of time."

R. M. Howes, M.D., Ph.D.

5/26/04

"In order for the body to maintain homeostatic normalcy,
it's self-contained, chemical-cornucopia must be stocked
piled
with the component curatives which constitute
a personal 'pharmacopoeia.'
We know this from observation,
yet, we tend to disavow its presence and
to ignore its impact.
And the wheel goes round in circles."

R. M. Howes, M.D., Ph.D.

8/23/04

"With regards to cancer and atherosclerosis, the
inflammatory cell has been convicted of guilt by association
and oxygen has been strung up by a rush-to-judgment
scientific lynch mob."

R. M. Howes, M.D., Ph.D.

5/9/04

"Fatuous condemnation of the beneficence of dioxygen,
is tantamount to
the evasion of sunshine
for fear of a longing to go out-of-doors,
to denouncing bodily nourishment
perchance for fear of choking and
to the damnation of love
for fear
of a broken heart."

R.M. Howes, M.D., Ph.D.

5/31/04

"The verity of the nature of oxygen radicals
can only be realized by acknowledgement of the condition
resultant to their absence: death and rigor mortis.
The way of the radical
is the way of life."

R. M. Howes, M.D., Ph.D.

6/11/04

"The electromagnetic puppeteer dictates the
cadence and thoughts of the aerobiotic legions."

R. M. Howes, M.D., Ph.D.

5/2/04

Whilst encased in our uterine cocoon,
as the cellular supernova of life begins,
we parasitically tap into Mom's oxygen supply
for perpetuated hits of this gaseous goody.
Thereafter, sleeping for over one third of our lives,
we robotically continuously suck in fresh crucial oxygen,
to feed our lifelong insatiable dioxygen addiction.
Even our thinking organ and our cells for thought,
need a nightly time out; but all the while, under the trusted
guidance of
an almighty auto-pilot.

R.M. Howes, M.D., Ph. D.

8/3/04

Great thoughts are a relative rarity;
whereas,
great mistakes are commonplace.

R. M. Howes, M.D., Ph.D.

8/19/04

"The metabolic rhythm of life, the harmony exhibited by
proteins, sugars, lipids and nucleic acids and
the diurnal anabolic cellular grind are prima facie evidence
of the presence of heretofore undefined and unidentified
powerfully precise primeval forces which have interacted to
propel
mankind's evolutionary launch."

R. M. Howes, M.D., Ph.D.

5/27/04

"Scare tactics of the oxy-morons have spawned a generation
of oxy-phobes, who believe that ground state oxygen, itself,
is a diabolical "toxin," which only acts as a
catabolic cellular assassin."

R. M. Howes, M.D., Ph. D.

5/9/04

"In searching for the road of truth, for the Free Radical
Theory of Aging and Oxidative stress, I found that it was
riddled with gaping paradoxical potholes of contradiction,
which rendered it impassable.
In fact, I found that this avenue to enlightenment
had been completely blockaded by bricks of biochemistry.
The theory had been distributed and taught from
a passage in the Great Book of
Medical Mythology, along with phlogistin,
spontaneous generation, thymic hypertrophy
and hormone replacement therapy."

R. M. Howes, M.D., Ph.D.

7/18/04

"Paper by paper, reference by reference, fact by fact,
I am going to paint you a scientific picture,
secure it in the gilded frame of the
Howes Unified Theory
and hang it over the entry door-pore
leading to the stunning
beauty of the intracellular labyrinth.
There, you may behold
the startling and mysterious vistas
of the naked human corpus."

R. M. Howes, M.D., Ph.D.

6/10/04

"Lascivious oxygen carries on curt, torrid affairs
with throngs of willing electrons,
whilst maintaining a most meaningful relationship
with its photon mate."

R. M. Howes, M.D., Ph.D.

5/23/04

"Some findings of greatness, occur by accident,
others by serendipity, whilst others require
nigh pathological levels
of progressive persistence from conception, to birth,
through growth and development.
Over two decades have passed since the seed of
the Howes Singlet Oxygen Delivery system germinated
in my frontal lobes, and now,
as muscular momentum of contractions build, my idea is
birthing.
I feel it,
and excitedly await its arrival,
so I can hear baby discovery's first joyous cry,
"Eureka."

R. M. Howes, M.D., Ph.D.

6/08/04

"Out of the compacted, fertile soil of controversy, will sprout the rose of the Howes Unified Theory, which will blossom above the specious weeds of the Free Radical Theory of Aging and Oxidative Stress."

R. M. Howes, M.D., Ph.D.

5/26/04

"Persistence transforms the weakling acorn into the mighty oak of the informed, which can withstand the wicked winds of ignorance throughout a storm of discovery and a vortex of controversy."

R. M. Howes, M.D., Ph.D.

5/3/04

"Learned authors bombastically state that
horrid oxygen radicals
wreak devastation and havoc upon defenseless DNA,
unprotected proteins, helpless unsaturated lipids and sugars
slowly self-destruct under oxygen's fatal influence.
Lethal oxygen joins hands with its demonic iron brethren
and ushers out the hydroxyl radical hit man, who is adept at
killing all in his path.
Yet,
life endures and thrives.
Now, you prophets of oxidative doom,
smile,
take a deep oxygen-breath and
go forth and prosper."

R. M. Howes, M.D., Ph.D.

6/11/04

"The nobility of oxygen has been smothered by
the suffocating smog emitted from putrid heaps of decaying
pseudoscientific publications."

R. M. Howes, M.D., Ph.D.

5/10/04

"Modern man arrives upon this earth hell-bent and hard-wired for:

oxygen consumption, for EMOD/excytomer production,
intellectual curiosity for fear of the unknown,
basic drives for pleasure and perpetuation of our unique
double helix,
an ability to create, equaled by a propensity to destroy,
a self-cure system coupled with a homeostatic over-ride,
compensatory religiosity for our sinful ways,
a fight or flight reflex which opposes societal regulation,
and an assured face-to-face rendezvous with the Reaper."

R.M. Howes, M.D., Ph.D.

8/24/04

Howes, R. M. *Hydrogen Peroxide: Monograph 1:
Scientific, Medical and Biochemical Overview &
Antioxidant Vitamins A, C & E: Monograph 2: Equivocal
Scientific Studies.* © 2006. Free Radical Publishing Co.
Kentwood, LA

As goes oxygen,
so goes the undulating waves of biota life forms,
clinging to our planet's fragile surface.
Life flourished during the oxygen-rich Triassic times
and die-offs paralleled spans of atmospheric hypoxia.
Oxygen is the brain's mate and the heart's mistress.
It is the lover to all aerobic cells.
The thought of anoxia is
"simply out of this world."

R.M. Howes M.D., Ph.D.

12/23/05

A life span passes with such rapidity
that, simply put, most of us
just plain ole' damn near miss it completely.

R. M. Howes, M.D., Ph.D.

9/27/09

There are no extraterrestrial beings
On Mars or the moon, because....
they are all on the sun!
Who do you think keeps the fire going?
This is the origin of the saying,
"Some like it hot."
Yeah, buddy.

R. M. Howes, M.D., Ph.D.

10/23/09

The complexities in the living/breathing cell
are light years removed
from the simplicity of test tube coffin studies,
which are clearly laden
with countless
"dead" artifacts.

R. M. Howes, M.D., Ph.D.

4/7/05

Fabricating crucial electronically modified oxygen derivatives,
the body's biochemical assembly line hums at
a hellacious nano-second pace,
whilst radicophobes filibuster their essentiality.
It is increasingly apparent
that the acuity of the mind's eye of the oxy-moron
is borderline blind.

R. M. Howes, M.D., Ph.D.

12/26/05

Howes, R.M.
Howes' Encyclopedia of Antioxidants (vitamins) and Reactive
Oxygen Species Insufficiency (ROSI) as the Basis for Disease
Allowance and Coexistence of Diseases:
Extraordinary Support for an Extraordinary Theory. Vol I-3.
© 2008.
Free Radical Publishing Co. Kentwood, LA

Dr. Harman,
"How could so many
have been so wrong
for so long?"

R. M. Howes, M.D., Ph.D.

6/6/06

Radicals and antioxidants are flip sides
of the same redox chemical coin.

R. M. Howes, M.D., Ph.D.

11/6/07

Extraordinary theories necessitate
extraordinary proof.
The free radical theory is falsified by a glut of
non-supportive, paradoxical, conflicting, confusing,
inconclusive evidence and a modicum of
supportive documentation.
It exhibits
extreme vulnerability as regards
its logicality.

R. M. Howes, M.D., Ph.D.

11/15/06

AH HA! Inc.

R. M. Howes, M.D., Ph.D.

9/17/06

Darwin's natural selection has morphed into
un-natural selection.
We can no longer hide from the Jeckel-Hyde reality.
Like a balloon clown, technology precariously
molds and folds
humankind's genetic helix into a nucleic acid
pretzel of its own choosing.
The fundamentals of evolution have been bypassed by
the white coated marauders manipulating white rats.
Extrapolating, we now have green pigs,
which glow in the dark,
riding along with us on our lonely little planet,
as we whizz through the universal expanse of fundamental
nothingness,
not aware that all may be
hopelessly diluted throughout the rarefied reality of infinity.
Hoo-fricking-ray, homo tecknapiens.

R. M. Howes, M.D., Ph.D.

5/17/06

We live as a collective organism,
which assembles its beautiful quidity
from vast numbers of cellular singularities
and a chorus of raised sub cellular organelle voices,
all trying to sing harmoniously
in the choir of life.

R. M. Howes, M.D., Ph.D.

11/21/06

Latin for poison…tuhdah…the VIRUS marauds.
Existent only for reproduction,
a truly singular purpose entity.
Capable of crystallizing during century-long dry spells,
it waits, patiently,
ever so patiently.
Multitudes and species variants
are specialized to hone in on specific organs and cells.
The biological equivalent of a smart bomb,
it waits for the kill.
Ever present in all living forms,
they attack with certitude, during periods of weakness.
Beware of the opening of Pandora's Box,
in the tropical rainforest,
for it harbors the relatives of HIV,
and their killing kin.

R. M. Howes, M.D., Ph.D.

5/30/06

Salk made polio balk.
Small pox, which duped Montezuma,
was cornered in Somalia and snuffed out.
Now, measles, mumps and influenza wait in fear,
as the laboratory egg hatches out batches of vaccine.
DNA viruses maintain elephantine memory but
its RNA cousins don many tricky disguises,
capable of stumping the sleuthing vaccine.
Pigs and ducks are the breweries that
yield new viral vintages annually.
Rotaviruses have established a battle ground
in the intestines of third world countries.
Hygeia,
please step forward to save the children.

R. M. Howes, M.D., Ph.D.

5/30/06

I was born with the Big Bang
but I have been around for a long time before that.
Fusion fathered me and fission was my mother.
I have kin scattered all over the cosmos
and I feel like I already know them and
would likely recognize them,
if I was to run into one of them
in the neighborhood cyclotron.
My home is in the Milky Way and I enjoy taking
light-year journeys within my mind.
Oxygen is my bestest friend.
I have a good yet fairly frenetic life,
generating ATP, metabolizing organics and
contemplating consciousness.
My essence has coalesced with eternity,
So, I'll probably see you there.
Best regards,
The Pundit.

R. M. Howes, M.D., Ph.D.

9/14/06

Constant vigilance against pathogens
is a requirement for prolonged aerobic organismal health.
Hordes of attackers lay in wait,
for relaxation of our oxidative capabilities,
such that oodles of these nefarious onlookers can do their
dirty work.

R. M. Howes, M.D., Ph.D.

9/21/06

Throughout recorded history,
man is the only species scampering
to participate in mass insanity...
alone or in groups,
over and over again.

R. M. Howes, M.D., Ph.D.

12/13/06

Ninety two year old Jack LaLanne
says that inactivity is death and that
exercise is life.
I say that this is so because of the copious amounts of
electronically modified oxygen derivatives (EMODs)
produced
during these work-out periods.
Exercise conjures up and brings forth
the magic of EMODs.

R. M. Howes, M.D., Ph.D.

11/23/06

Science may be a psychological coping mechanism
whereby we pretend to partially understand
the inexplicable and incomprehensible complexities of life
and the anticipated, unfathomable specter concerning
death.
It provides so little solace
to succor scientists that they are scared
out of their virtual senses.

R. M. Howes, M.D., Ph.D.

7/15/06

Many authors speak of a tortuously slow
corrosive oxidation of the body.
Yet, the fundamental place that I see decomposition
is throughout the supportive infrastructure
of the free radical theory.
Failed predictions have rusted away
any columns of credibility
and left behind an eroded pile
of tarnished confusion.

R.M. Howes M.D., Ph.D.

12/27/06

Hostility reigns in the observable universe.
Climaxing in an annihilation crescendo,
matter and anti-matter are driven to mutual destruction,
only to be born again.
On our planet, layer upon species-layer of biota
acts out the play entitled, "Eat or be eaten."
Deep within our biological quantum cosmos,
the program is re-titled, "Oxidize or be oxidized."
Kidnap an electron
and a proton will follow or vice versa,
but keep the flow moving, for it is this movement
which engenders the life force and
begets Change,
and thusly coaxes along her ugly twin sister, Aging.
So,......
deal with it, Dahlin'.

R. M. Howes, M.D., Ph.D.

10/1/06

With collision analysis, we struggle to determine
the inner working quantum characteristics of the atom
and its subatomic clan.
Fission, fusion and scatter have yielded scant knowledge
of their non-Newtonian world.
Yet, even the slightest of these particles
knows all of the inherent quantum laws and follows them explicitly.
They have demonstrated this to us in the box-car letters,
spelled out on the periodic table.
Their distinctive behavior demonstrates
their inherently distinctive knowledge.
They are the site of the cognitive atomic and
molecular thinking matrix, which dictates
the habits of the world,
and which envelops all.

R. M. Howes, M.D., Ph.D.

11/15/06

Memory is an approximation only.
The recipe of recall is made with a
dash of facts, a pinch of fantasy and
a smidgen of fabrication....and
don't you forget it.

R. M. Howes, M.D., Ph.D.

1/08/07

"You are being radically misled
by antioxidant vitamin fraudsters."
Someone is trying to radically mislead you
concerning antioxidant vitamins and
antioxidant supplements,
such that you will make
a radical mistake."

R.M. Howes M.D., Ph.D.

3/22/06

The spurious free radical theory, invalidated and not genuine,
is an insular example of ignorance in action.

R. M. Howes, M.D., Ph.D.

1/17/07

Life is designed such that
human perfection is
never-ever obtainable.

R. M. Howes, M.D., Ph.D.

1/19/07

Stronger than kryptonite,
mightier than uranium,
more powerful than refined plutonium,
it stands alone.
It is....
TESTOSTERONE, the almighty.
Trust me, I know what I am talking about.
Just ask your ex....or Tiger Woods.

R. M. Howes, M.D., Ph.D.

12/4/09

The free radi-crap theory is
the dropped end product of
Kerplunk Sphincteric Productions.

R. M. Howes, M.D., Ph.D.

12/12/09

Life is just too damned crazy,
too strange, too weird,
to be....real.
Really,.... it is!

R. M. Howes, M.D., Ph.D.

12/13/09

If life is real,
likely, so is death and
that is even....crazier.

R. M. Howes, M.D., Ph.D.

12/13/09

Hiding in plain sight
is the glorious fact that oxygen
protects and sustains us.
As happens all too often, we are blinded
by the obvious.

R. M. Howes, M.D., Ph.D.

1/19/07

If the free radical theory had been a horse,
it would now be glue.

R. M. Howes, M.D., Ph.D.

1/13/07

Knowing the truth
beats living in blissful ignorance
every time.

R. M. Howes, M.D., Ph.D.

4/10/07

I can change the world,
if I can get its attention and
if I can get my theories acted upon.

R. M. Howes, M.D., Ph.D.

4/15/07

All humans may be versions of Adam and Eve
and you and I may be versions of each other.
Yet, we muster change and variability
to produce a resilient spectrum of individuality
from criminals to saints,
from geniuses to idiots,
and from the one known as "me"
to the one known as "you" .
Life is "way cool."

R. M. Howes, M.D., Ph.D.

6/17/07

For the maudlin,
oxygenology is radicalicious.
Yet, over consumption can lead to
morbid O_2besity.

R. M. Howes, M.D., Ph.D.

6/30/07

Other than the fact that it has been
discredited, refuted, invalidated, disproved, rebutted and
negated,
deluded experts believe that the free radical theory
seemingly holds great promise
in the treatment of over 200 diseases
and for the reversal of aging.
Puhleeze....get educated, you clowns.
Stop the tomfoolery.

R. M. Howes, M.D., Ph.D.

7/03/07

Following fertilization, the embryo/fetus complex
performs unbelievably complex sequences of synthesis.
The developing cellular, molecular and atomic components
seemingly operate with a level of precision,
which supercedes perfunctory processes and
exhibits an acumen consistent with wisdom and intelligence.
Thus, the astuteness of molecules and atoms is established.
Yet, like our brains,
they do not always make the right decision or
chose the correct course of action.
C'est la vie.

R. M. Howes, M.D., Ph.D.

7/06/07

Life is a biochemically and electronically
strenuous and stress-filled process.

R. M. Howes, M.D., Ph.D.

8/13/07

Overall, humans appear to accept death
as they near their inescapable fate.
It appears that after enduring the travails of Job,
their demise is not nearly as distasteful,
as during their times of youthful indiscretions.
Whilst multiple organs increasingly dysfunction,
the eternal respite
is increasingly palatable.
Naked you came and naked
Ye' shall return,
but I will take my knowledge with me.
In the vernacular of 21st century youth,
"Holy Moley, Dude,
it kinda' sounds like
"Death is a dead certainty."

R. M. Howes, M.D., Ph.D.

9/23/07

Unfounded rhetoric extolling the wonders of antioxidants
sucks all of the oxygen from the air.
Shud'up, already!

R. M. Howes, M.D., Ph.D.

10/14/07

Leo Tolstoy said, "It is amazing how complete
the delusion that beauty is goodness."
I say, "It is amazing how complete the delusion
that antioxidants are goodness."
Great minds run in the same
biochemical pathways.

R. M. Howes, M.D., Ph.D.

10/14/07

Antioxidants are free radicals
in sheep's clothing.
These free radical, disguised precursors sneak around
pretending to be unlike the oxidant-wolf
but they equally enjoy feasting on a bloody electron
exchange.
Peel back their sheep skin
and there stands a naked radical.
It is what sustains the nature
and the essence of life.

R. M. Howes, M.D., Ph.D.

11/6/07

Antioxidants are claimed to be free radical scavengers
but they are only "biochemical buzzards."
They circle overhead sniffing out
the decaying carcasses of free radical soldiers
that have fallen in combat with pathogens.
They kill the weaker oxidant-militants
and dine on the carnage of their battles.
Pathetic!

R. M. Howes, M.D., Ph.D.

11/6/07

Test tube biochemical experiments utilize a dead gumbo;
whereas, the breathing human body
is a miraculous, functioning complex
of compartmentalization,
with instantaneous inter- and intra-cellular cross talk,
demonstrating the amazing ability of self control.
No wonder we can not generalize the result of one to the other.
Scientists attempt to compare two different beasts:
one, living and the other, dead
and express dismay when their results do not extrapolate.
Can the professed brilliant really
be that dumb?
So,…….. go figure.

R. M. Howes, M.D., Ph.D.

11/6/07

Spurious statistical associations
are the malodorous herring,
which confound the
scientific hounds and completely throw them off of the
sweet-smelling trail of truth.
The stench of the putrid misleading misinformation
is nigh unbearable.

R. M. Howes, M.D., Ph.D.

11/12/07

Myths frequently smother facts and
mendacity strangles veracity.
It requires incredible persistence and courage
to expose and teach truth.
In the areas of dietary supplementation and medicine,
data undergoes daily manipulation
to promote "sales based on pseudoscience"
and "profit based on lies."

R. M. Howes, M.D., Ph.D.

11/22/07

Aerobic organisms pose as biochemical Petri dishes
for the study of oxygen metabolism.
We must swirl the dish contents
and try to read the "radical" tea leaves for the future,
....all,
for the betterment of mankind.

R. M. Howes, M.D., Ph.D.

6/10/07

The big bang vs. the steady state model of
cosmological origin.
Which is right?
I say that, "All that is,
always was and always will be."
Naturally, the steady state wins.

R. M. Howes, M.D., Ph.D.

1/3/08

Customarily, we do not die all at once.
We die in pieces, little by little.
First, the blood vessels of the heart and the brain go.
Concurrently, the lungs lose functionality and
oxygen delivery throughout the body declines,
as we slowly suffocate in the open air.
Muscle mass dwindles, whilst the high school hunk morphs
into a walking adipocyte.
Vision squints, as silence settles in the ears.
All the while, the plaques thicken and
the cancerous crab scoots freely about and breeds.
Hail, hail, the death gang is all here
to sing the final verse of life.
Peace be with you,
"a little piece at a time."

R. M. Howes, M.D., Ph.D.

1/3/08

As a species, we suffer mass amnesia
of all of our previous lives.
How quickly we forget.

R. M. Howes, M.D., Ph.D.

1/3/08

Subatomic particles act as cellular carrier pigeons.
Protons and electrons dart and fly around,
whilst broadcasting messages and all the while
they chirp the songs of life.

R. M. Howes, M.D., Ph.D.

1/22/08

Invisible millions inhabit our planet
performing only perfunctory dietary and defacatory acts.
They possess no means of influencing the evolutionary
direction
of their species.
Corporate power brokers and political operatives
pull the strings of societal change.
Most people are relegated to quite,
meaningless, passive lives.
Oh, well....

R. M. Howes, M.D., Ph.D.

2/10/08

The length,
depth and exquisite detail of my work
makes it nigh impenetrable and
assures me that it is highly unlikely
to be read by my contemporaries,
who are hopelessly biased,
marginally scientifically literate,
abstract-reading, so-called....
investigators.

R. M. Howes, M.D., Ph.D.

4/21/08

To clearly see the mysterious cosmic wonders,
which appear to invisibly interlink
the atom and the universe
or the cell and the cosmos,
with never-before realized clarity,
simply open wide
your mind's eye.

R. M. Howes, M.D., Ph.D.

4/26/08

Queries concerning our previous lives and
speculations on our unspecified programmed deaths
are just too damn personal
to discuss.

R. M. Howes, M.D., Ph.D.

5/09/08

All past scientists and aging gurus,
who claimed to know the answer to aging and
who came up with their ideas over 60 years ago,
have been shown to be
"dead wrong."
Their erroneous notions are
spelled out on their headstones.

R. M. Howes, M.D., Ph.D.

5/14/08

The late Robert F. Kennedy said, "Few are willing to brave the
disapproval of their colleagues, the wrath of their society.
Moral courage is a rarer commodity than bravery in battle
or great intelligence.
Yet, it is the one essential vital quality for those who seek to
change
a world that yields the most painfully to change."
So it is with opponents of the free radical theory,
who have been besmirched by theory sycophants
with great "radicule."

R. M. Howes, M.D., Ph.D.

5/15/08

I once woke up from a hangover so bad,
that I had
blood-shot hair.
Bottoms up, boys.

R. M. Howes, M.D., Ph.D.

5/15/08

The free radical theory of disease and aging
is utterly
"radiculous."

R. M. Howes, M.D., Ph.D.

5/16/08

Aristotle said, "Nature does nothing uselessly."
I say, "Nature is a curious combination
of chaos and complexity of design,
resulting in perpetuation
and improvement of function."
Remember, many things appear to be
by intelligent intent but
some things just "are."

R. M. Howes, M.D., Ph.D.

8/20/08

We arise from the cosmos
and we will be resorbed by the cosmos....
over and over again.
Maybe eventually
we will get it
right.

R. M. Howes, M.D., Ph.D.

10/14/08

The sculptors of organized medicine
have chiseled out their ersatz image
with mythic properties and biblical proportions.
Yet, with all of their hammering
on the stone of human perception,
they have failed to carry a single patient's life into....
perpetuity.
So, heal thyself, physician.
Heal thyself of a lethal case of
uber-hubris.

R. M. Howes, M.D., Ph.D.

5/18/08

The unpredictable free radical theory
has never "radisfied" the requirements of the
scientific method,
at least, not to my
"radisfaction."

R. M. Howes, M.D., Ph.D.

7/6/08

Howes, R.M. *Diabetes and Oxygen Free Radical Sophistry.*
© 2006. Free Radical Publishing Co. Kentwood, LA

Free radical activity has been blamed
for chaotic, cellular, cumulative, molecular damage.
Yet, I do not see a constant place for chaos
in the magnificently choreographed course
of a propagating living/breathing cell.
Chaos equates to entropic death and
death is a self-limiting event,
i.e., a suicidal-thinning of the herd.
Apoptosis follows its instinctual leader and
obediently carries out its death march
to the tune of the biochemical drummer.

R. M. Howes, M.D., Ph.D.

5/11/05

If one were to pull the thread
of a singular biochemical pathway,
you would inadvertently tug on
the totality of the living cellular fabric.

R. M. Howes, M.D., Ph.D.

9/21/06

A state of health is only maintained
by a continuously vigilant oxidative defensive system,
without which we quickly succumb to
bugs, drugs and thugs called cancer cells.
Debilities and anomalies of our somatic condition are
pounced upon by pathogens and mutagens
but they are quickly
"rebuffed by radicals."
Oxidative "radical outbursts" of EMODs
are proven tireless workers.
So it is in the world of
homeostasis.

R. M. Howes, M.D., Ph.D.

6/11/06

The voracious vortex of the free radical theory
has sucked up the common sense of medical biochemistry.
This anomaly of logic posits the artifice that
oxygen is the primary instrument of the Grim Reaper and
that it is the root system from which sprouts nigh all
pathophysiologies.
Author after author acquiesces to this cheap parlor trick and
appears blind to this scientific sleight of hand.
I beg you to look around at the beauty of aerobic nature,
take a deep breath, relax and reconsider.
Oxygen is the indispensable energy ingredient,
sustaining the magic and mystery
of all human experiences.
It is self evident.

R. M. Howes, M.D., Ph.D.

5/21/06

Howes, R.M. *"The Medical and Scientific Significance of Oxygen Free Radical Metabolism"* © 2005. Free Radical Publishing Co. Kentwood, LA

"The master's guard dogs were characterized
as pernicious, rapacious and only capable of
uncontrollable violence.
Yet, they only acted instinctively, with the innate loyalty of
an ever-dedicated protector.
And, so it is, with the
maligned reactive oxygen species;
truly, man's best friend."

R. M. Howes, M.D., Ph.D.

11/25/04

"O_2, and its kindred, stand as the singular barrier
between health and sepsis,
between normal and cancerous,
between living and dead.
This astonishing anomaly, of the periodic table,
offers unsolicited chemical solace
to the vulnerable collective of living creatures.
Thank you, most beloved
oxygen."

R. M. Howes, M.D., Ph.D.

11/25/04

"The unparalleled arrogance of medical scientists,
in pretending to understand the overwhelming intricacies
of the living/breathing cell,
is as extreme as is the extent of my being humbled by its
unbelievably beautiful complexities
and its instinctive wisdom."

R. M. Howes, M.D., Ph.D.

1/10/05

You or I, as a distinct organism,
may represent a cumulative puppet,
displaying the antics, desires and drives of our
lesser molecular and atomic constituents;
for better or worse, for richer or poorer and
in sickness or in biochemical homeostasis.
Yes, it's a heavenly molecular marriage.

R. M. Howes, M.D., Ph.D.

5/12/05

Classical oxygen and its free radical offspring
are the cross-pollinating butterflies of biological molecules,
which transfer exponential numbers of sweet electrons.
They are the skillful molecular humming birds,
acrobatically darting to-and-fro to obtain their
fill of electron-nectar.
They are the colorful honey bees of aerobic life,
busily buzzing to overcome adversity and to endure.
They are the cellular pony-express,
lathered and riding hard
to furnish intricate lines of intra-organismal communication
necessary to sustain living animation.

R. M. Howes, M.D., Ph.D.

5/26/05

"Once the novelty of 'free radical bashing' wears off,
one is struck by the obvious truth of oxygen's greatness.
It starts as a quasi-reactive ground state and
ends as reduced and non-reactive water,
such that all of its life-giving magic lies
within its electronic structure
in the 'realm of the radical'.
The mindless fun of the free radical theory of aging
and oxidative stress
is as meaningless as the
moon-howling,
of the peyote coyote."

R. M. Howes, M.D., Ph.D.

1-13-05

"The breath of life provides the heightened consciousness
of man, which enables us to achieve
the ecstasies of thought and caring.
Oxygen is sprinkled aplenty throughout our bodies'
phosphates, nitrates, hydroxides and sulphates,
totaling more than all other elements combined.
It is entwined with our DNA /RNA, where it is interwoven into
its sugared backbone and its hand-holding base pairs,
ultimately and romantically expressing itself as the love of
life.
Remove it
and love is gone, along with life."

R. M. Howes, M.D., Ph.D.

1/9/05

"Again and over and over again,
application of the free radical theory of aging
and oxidative stress
fails miserably to curtail man's misery.
Yet, the blind-believers bow, at the illusory altar
of Harman and Ames, praying that the holy antioxidants
will prevent and cure them of their ills....
with no relief in sight,
for their leaders have deceived them.
The antioxidant faithful have only been given the
poisoned pabulum of the party line.
Hearken, do not despair.
Summarily, truth is being shaken and aroused
from its fifty year trance...
by Howes."

R. M. Howes, M.D., Ph.D.

12/12/04

Thermodynamics' second law is wrong.
The life force proliferates with ever increasing levels of complexity.
In our sector of the universe,
order is being propagated in an inverted,
growing pyramidal pattern
by generational increments of assemblage.
On earth, time's arrow is shot from the bow
of the living and
is not carried in the quiver of Chaos.

R. M. Howes, M.D., Ph.D.

5/29/05

"Considered by the medical minions to be the most
destructive component affecting the cell,
oxygen radicals go about their
assigned diurnal nano-ceutical tasks.
They, being only momentarily withheld from
the precious oxygen-addicted neurons,
precipitously results in stroke;
whereas, oxygen devouring myocardial cells
keel over with rapid demise, in even the briefest absence
of life rendering, radical producing oxygen.
Now, fool, just try to convince the brain, the heart and me,
of the alleged, unequaled toxicity of
oxygen and its brethren."

R. M. Howes, M.D., Ph.D.

11/25/04

"Oxygen, the ingenious molecule."

R. M. Howes, M.D., Ph.D.

11/26/04

"The massive and muscular poly-pharmacy snake,
drives its shiny fangs through the patient's wallet
and deep into its prey's pale, quivering, and sickened flesh.
It writhes, whist pumping its synthesized venom
throughout the victims vascular tree.
Poisoned blood cells and neurons succumb,
with convulsive attempts to live,
but in the end
the serpent of profit always seems to win."

R. M. Howes, M.D., Ph.D.

12/18/04

"Beyond mysticism, beyond blind faith,
lies the universal reality, the reality of chaos
intermixed with order,
the reality of being, the reality of knowing and the
reality of living.
For there is the realm of the Guiding Hand,
which allows death to masquerade as an end,
which permits matter to pretend to be energy,
which requires the yin to embrace the yang
and which empowers the rapture and the joy of it all.
It is that which defines all parameters of the ultimate truth.
Know it. Accept it. Love it,
for there is
nothing else."

R. M. Howes, M.D., Ph.D.

1-13-05

"Dubbing something a therapy
does not render it harmless and
calling something else a medicine
does not guarantee its non-toxicity.
Far too frequently, both prove to be lethal and
cumulatively, they account for more deaths than all wars
combined.
Healer, take heed that your so-called cures
are not more deadly than
the diseases you so proudly profess to treat,
Mister Millennial Medicine Man."

R. M. Howes, M.D., Ph.D.

12/19/04

"Legislating healthcare is more aptly called
legislating wealth care.
The pharmaceuticide-fox now owns
the congressional hen house.
The consumer FDA's checks and balances now assures
Big Pharma fat checks and growing bottom-line balances.
Adverse drug reactions can be held in secret and
full disclosure is becoming a distant and fading dream.
As the drug industry breathes in more strengthening profits,
its groping tentacles embrace more politicians,
whilst its suckers sap out patient's life forces.
Uncontrolled powers and unbridled greed
scurry to cover and enwrap the global face of mankind and
to asphyxiate any and all opposition."

R. M. Howes, M.D., Ph.D.

12/19/04

"The luminosity of the cellular soul is
a reflection of singlet oxygen's photon fire core,
with which it will shed its light into the mind's dark recesses
and betwixt the brain's dimly-lit convolutions;
thus, it spreads its warmth
throughout the entirety and interstices of the body.
The spirituality of oxygen's chemiluminescence and its
exothermicity is ensconced in its ubiquity.
Frequently, the answers to life's greatest mysteries
have been cloaked right before our very eyes
all the while.
Oh, Blind One, open your eyes but more importantly,
open your mind's eye."

R. M. Howes, M.D., Ph.D.

1/9/05

"Following man's half century
of hyped antioxidant supplement consumption,
aging's course has continued unabated, as does 100+
diseases
attributed to oxygen free radicals.
Although it offers pseudo-solace to throngs of oxy-morons,
serial study failures, highlight the glaring fatuity
of the faux-scientific Free Radical theory.
Its transparencies have been held before the light
of singlet oxygen's photon illumination
and its hole-riddled, lifeless corpus is exposed.
With 20/20 hindsight and with unpredictably
scrawled all over it,
it should have been pronounced
DOA in the 20th century."

R. M. Howes, M.D., Ph.D.

12/21/04

"Increasingly, the pharmaceuticide-wolf is dressed in the
sheep-white lab coat of the
modern physician,
who shepards his sickly-flock."

R. M. Howes, M.D., Ph.D.

8/17/04

"Following vigorous promotion,
synthesized chemical concoctions are being poured
willy-nilly down the gaping gullets of
the naïve modern day medical consumer,
who consumes these toxins with blissful, Pac-man ignorance.
With splendiferous profits and veiled cure-claims,
Big Pharma whimsically denies responsibility
for adverse drug reactions
and for their own callous offenses.
Meanwhile, the peddlers of drugs declared, with a scheming snicker,
"Pay me handsomely for my potions and you will be
healthy, wealthy and wise…..Hee, hee, hee.
Trust me."

R. M. Howes, M.D., Ph.D.

12/14/04

Neoplasia is the ultimate, grandiose opportunist.
Like its chemical viral kin, it feeds off of its host,
till its parasitic extremes
silence the obliging hand that had fed it.
It lies in prolonged waiting, hidden in the deep, shadowy
recesses
of the cell's complex biochemical engine room.
Then, in a moment of prooxidant weakness,
it lethally crawls forth from its hiding place
to selfishly do its dirty work.
Spider venom-like, it gradually digests
its host-victim,
whilst deliriously cloning itself.
Its job is now done.
Its destiny is now realized.

R. M. Howes, M.D., Ph.D.

6/12/05

The "sick-o-phants" of the free radical theory of
disease and aging just released their latest dictum:
'Earth is the universal killer.'
They reason thusly,
all known creatures and critters
that have ever developed disease,
ever aged or ever died,
were exposed to fatal earth.....and
of course, logically they are right.
Unfortunately, the only grey matter these morons
have is that which they picked from their
noses.
Ewweehh!

R. M. Howes, M.D., Ph.D.

8/1/08

Howes, R.M. *"The Oxypocalypse: The war that never
happened" Reactive Oxygen Species Vs. Antioxidants"* ©
2009. Free Radical Publishing Co. Kentwood, LA.

The magnanimous dance of the redox electron
is the bona fide ballet of life.

R. M. Howes M.D., Ph.D.

11/18/08

Without educating the "radically" ignorant,
convincing them of the dangers of antioxidant overuse
is an impossibility.

R. M. Howes M.D., Ph.D.

11/18/08

Resolving redox confusion has proven
fiendishly difficult.

R. M. Howes M.D., Ph.D.

11/21/08

The most important of all rules
is the rule that
no rule is immutable or
put another way,
the rule is that no rule remains the same rule….
forever.
Rules are progressive
and not everlasting.

R. M. Howes M.D., Ph.D.

11/22/08

When the expanding universe collapses,
we may experience
reverse evolution
or "devil-ution."

R. M. Howes M.D., Ph.D.

11/22/08

Two main quarries, oxidants and antioxidants,
supply the major building blocks
for electron and proton flow
in living entities.
Rock on!

R. M. Howes M.D., Ph.D.

11/23/08

Just about the time you begin to figure out life,
it's time to die
and you grasp just how little
you have figured out.

R. M. Howes M.D., Ph.D.

11/24/08

Just when you figure out that you can not
figure out life,
is when you realize that
we are all as dumb as a box of roxs….er, rocks.

R. M. Howes M.D., Ph.D.

11/28/08

"Antioxivores, gobble down
your synthetic supplements to
support billion dollar sales but
do so at your own peril.

R. M. Howes M.D., Ph.D.

12/18/08

Oxidants and antioxidants are like Wasabi or
a bass player---
i.e., they do not work well alone.
They are co-dependent in their life-sustaining quest
of promoting electron and proton flow.

R. M. Howes M.D., Ph.D.

1/8/09

The half century occurrence of the free radical theory
will merely represent a moment of confusion
in the overall history of redox thought,
aerobiosis and
oxygen appreciation.

R. M. Howes M.D., Ph.D.

1/19/09

Radicophobes can ignore the truth or
they can reject the truth but
they can not change the maginificent truths
regarding the crucial role
of EMODs in the life process
of all aerobes
or the inherent splendor of oxygen.

R. M. Howes M.D., Ph.D.

1/26/09

Under abnormal conditions,
electronically modified oxygen derivatives
may be toxic in excess but
the same can be said for water and food.
So?

R. M. Howes M.D., Ph.D.

2/5/09

Friends do not let friends
injudiciously ingest antioxidants.

R. M. Howes M.D., Ph.D.

2/11/09

Amused and annoyed in equal measure,
I peruse the antioxidant vitamin ads.
Quotes are inspired by the marketing and business milieu,
which distort the facts to score a selling point....
so much for science.
Let's hear it for sales.

R. M. Howes M.D., Ph.D.

2/11/09

I toil to reveal the deceptive profit-driven agenda
of the
antioxivores and radicophobes.

R. M. Howes M.D., Ph.D.

2/11/09

The best thing about the free radical theory
is that you intuitively feel and
instinctively know that it is wrong,...
just plain old wrong.

R. M. Howes M.D., Ph.D.

2/11/09

Antioxidants: known harm for unknown benefit.

R. M. Howes M.D., Ph.D.

2/11/09

Comprehensive
Rejuvenating
Antioxidant
Program:
C.R.A.P.
Yes, this is their antiaging plan.
There are CRAP creams, CRAP pills, CRAP supplements,
CRAP shampoos, etc.
In short,
it's all a lot of CRAP.

R. M. Howes M.D., Ph.D.

2/22/09

Hydrogen and oxygen are two of the
most flammable elements.
Yet, combine them into water and
they are a most effective extinguisher of their own fire.
The very essence of nature can be drastically altered
by associations and the company we keep.

R. M. Howes M.D., Ph.D.

2/28/09

Oxygen is the biomarker for life
on planet Earth and used as such
by those in the search
of life throughout the universe.
It is not the sentinel of death,
as espoused
by the ersatz free radi-crap theory.

R. M. Howes M.D., Ph.D.

3/28/09

Many faux theorist on aging
subscribe to the free radical theory,
which is like the theory of Bigfoot,
only with less credibility or substance.

R. M. Howes M.D., Ph.D.

3/28/09

Faith is the capacity of accepting, without question,
the incomprehensible as acknowledged
and simplified facts.

R. M. Howes M.D., Ph.D.

5/9/09

Theorists propose a multiplicity of parallel universes.
I have visited them many times.
I sleep
and enter via the dream-worm-hole portal.
It is as real as all of the other unprovable universes.
The dream dimension truly alters space and time
in a remarkable, mysterious
and inexplicable manner.

R. M. Howes M.D., Ph.D.

5/19/09

Humans are being rejected by the planet.
I feel it.

R. M. Howes M.D., Ph.D.

6/8/09

At 65, I have entered a strange place.
A place of looming questions and a
place where I realize that
I am nearer to death than I am
to life.
I am no longer all here,
parts of the whole have been lost
after passing my peak.
It is mucho unsettling.
Comprende?

R. M. Howes M.D., Ph.D.

6/22/09

Certain self evident truths
need not require additional evidence or proof,
such as the low toxicity of EMODs,
as evidenced by their omnipresent ubiquity.

R. M. Howes M.D., Ph.D.

7/15/09

I believe that nature is composed of infinitely complex
related factoids (convoluted factual cousins),
each of which contains Byzantine elements beyond our
realm of comprehension.

R. M. Howes M.D., Ph.D.

7/15/09

Based on the "design follows function" principle,
one should not be surprised
when a thing does what it was designed to do,
such as a radical seeking an electron or
a man seeking a woman or
of a woman satisfying a man.

One can not change the character of a thing
unless you permanently change
its basic nature,
human nature or
Mother Nature.

R. M. Howes M.D., Ph.D.

7/20/09

Howes, R.M. *"Radically Change Your Thinking About Oxygen"*
© 2010. Free Radical Publishing Co. Kentwood, LA.

Life.... strange life,
is being forced to play a lead role
in a Stephen King novella.
Logic is lost,
firm conclusions are nowhere to be found and
you end up unsettled and frightened
by his monstrous yarn.
BOO!!
Scared ya' didn't I.

R. M. Howes, M.D., Ph.D.

9/7/09

The God that I know is not bearded
nor slumped into a golden throne.
Rather, it is a universally pervasive "enabling presence,"
which encourages order
but does not demand it,
which makes subtle suggestions
without dictates and
which has no problem leaving questions
unanswered or requests unfulfilled.
It's simply.... that complex.

R. M. Howes, M.D., Ph.D.

9/7/09

Scientific inquiry can never be completed,
only extended.

R. M. Howes, M.D., Ph.D.

9/7/09

Experience is the primo teacher,
enlightening us as to how little we really know.

R. M. Howes, M.D., Ph.D.

9/7/09

The less you know,
the less you question.

R. M. Howes, M.D., Ph.D.

9/7/09

To put one's faith in people
is to seek disappointment.
To put one's faith in ideas of discovery
is to be pestered by never-ending curiosity.

R. M. Howes, M.D., Ph.D.

9/7/09

I am driven by an intriguing need
to find answers for mankind.
Thus, the quest never ends and
true satiety can never be realized.

R. M. Howes, M.D., Ph.D.

9/7/09

The principled mind will follow
its instinctual hunches till
its very last synapse.
Satisfaction comes
in the pursuit of doing.

R. M. Howes, M.D., Ph.D.

9/7/09

The present, momentarily stabilizes me
in the current of the stream of time.
Otherwise, I am perpetually adrift.

R. M. Howes, M.D., Ph.D.

9/7/09

The mind is fortified by learning
and the spirit is strengthened by doing.
Combined, they become exponential.

R. M. Howes, M.D., Ph.D.

9/7/09

The human body is simultaneously
a masterpiece of energy and
a mysterious miracle of matter.
It does and it thinks.

R. M. Howes, M.D., Ph.D.

9/7/09

In the sewer of universal facts,
I only seek to grasp turds of truth,
bobbling amongst the multitude of fictitious floaters.
At best, the grueling labor still stinks.

R. M. Howes, M.D., Ph.D.

9/7/09

Nature's inherent push
is driven by oxygen's search
for fulfillment.

R. M. Howes, M.D., Ph.D.

9/7/09

The disciplined and virtuous life
is an honored life.

R. M. Howes, M.D., Ph.D.

9/7/09

Every human body has a cure inside it
and it is my scientific task to discover it.

R. M. Howes, M.D., Ph.D.

9/7/09

I despise precious time wasted,
for it alone, is the unfinished canvas
displaying the portrait of my life.

R. M. Howes, M.D., Ph.D.

9/7/09

The living/breathing cell holds within it
the answers to every query
the physician can ever perceive or fathom.
He struggles to tease out its secret cures,
whilst the scientist suffers to know "why?"

R. M. Howes, M.D., Ph.D.

9/7/09

Although I speak of atomic particles as prime movers,
it must never be forgotten
that all reactions are driven by
pulses, charges or fields of energy.
Some attract, some repel.
Some love, some hate.
It can build or it can destroy.
You and I are collectives of energy,
which are manifested by our matter complement.
Energy perfects our quiddity.
It defines our lives....
and our loves.
Damn, that is touching.

R. M. Howes, M.D., Ph.D.

9/7/09

Water, water everywhere.
Wow. We seemed to have missed it
in biological class discussions.
Yet, it is the mothered milieu of living matter,
the scaffold-matrix of organic constituents,
the great proton carrier,
a storehouse for oxygen
and the brainchild of an energy-idea.

R. M. Howes, M.D., Ph.D.

9/7/09

I have a burning combustive love of oxygen
deep inside of me.
Honestly, I do....
and so do you.

R. M. Howes, M.D., Ph.D.

9/10/09

In my editorials regarding out-of-control Big Pharma,
I merely represent an annoying chigger attacking
the dangling, sweaty scrotum of a gargantuan elephant.
I can't really hurt it but,
assuredly,
I can irritate the hell out of it.

R. M. Howes, M.D., Ph.D.

9/20/09

In trying to turn opinion on disease allowance
and coexistence,
I appear to be a petite Louisiana blue crab pushing
furiously against the bow of the lumbering QE2,
trying frantically to change its direction....
to keep it from hitting the upcoming shoals of
misinformation.
By the tested laws of physics,
I can amend its course
but it is going to require that my
diminutive flippers move faster than
a redox electron.
In other words,
I've got to swim like hell.

R. M. Howes, M.D., Ph.D.

9/20/09

Perhaps I have focused too much on tomorrow
throughout my life,
thus, overlooking and not fully appreciating
the all important now.

R. M. Howes, M.D., Ph.D.

9/12/09

An the end of the short span of the next 100 years,
you and I and all of the people that you and I
know and love will all be dead,
as will be all of the creatures and
critters that live along side us
and occupy this coincidental slot in the
wave of existence.

R. M. Howes, M.D., Ph.D.

9/12/09

The only oxygen we need is
one pint per breath at the rate of
only a minimum of 21,600 times per day.
Other than that....

R. M. Howes, M.D., Ph.D.

9/12/09

Man:
The planet's craziest critter.

R. M. Howes, M.D., Ph.D.

9/14/09

Privately,
everyone is a little bonkers,
the proof of which
you hide in your dreams
and fantasies....
If any doubts, just check out
the evening news.

R. M. Howes, M.D., Ph.D.

9/14/09

www.ingramcontent.com/pod-product-compliance
Lightning Source LLC
Chambersburg PA
CBHW031237280526
45784CB00004B/1608